Big Boss

BIG BOSS

by Anne Rockwell

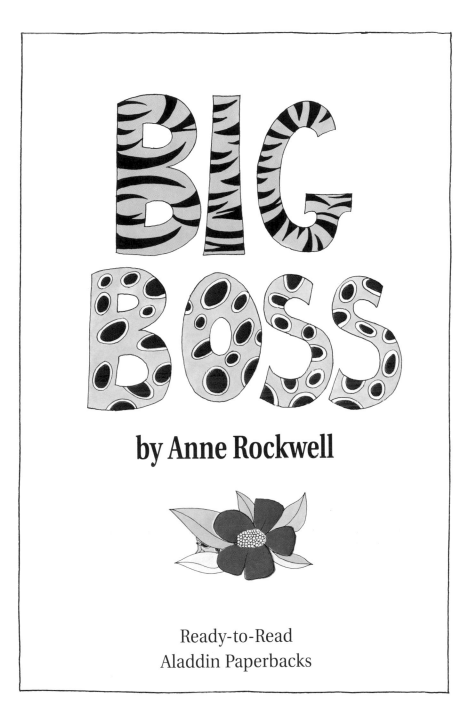

Ready-to-Read
Aladdin Paperbacks

First Aladdin Paperbacks Edition, 1987
Copyright © 1975 by Anne Rockwell

Aladdin Paperbacks
An imprint of Simon & Schuster Children's Publishing Division
1230 Avenue of the Americas
New York, NY 10020

READY-TO-READ is a registered trademark of Simon & Schuster, Inc.
Also available in a Simon & Schuster Books for Young Readers Edition.

Printed and bound in the United States of America
10 9 8 7 6 5 4 3 2 1

The Library of Congress has cataloged the hardcover edition as follows:

Rockwell, Anne F. Big Boss.
Reprint. Originally published: New York: Macmillan, 1975.
Summary: Relates how a clever little frog outwits a tiger and a fox.
[1. Frogs—Fiction. 2. Animals—Fiction] I. Title
[PZ7.R5943Bi 1987] [E] 86-22230
ISBN 0-689-80883-6 (hc)   0-689-80884-4 (pbk)

For Hannah,
Elizabeth
and Oliver

Contents

The Hungry Tiger   9

The Jump   17

The Winner   29

The Fox   41

Time for Dinner   55

The Hungry Tiger

A tiger walked in the forest.
He sniffed and looked,
and looked and sniffed again.
Then he growled and said,
"I am a big, hungry tiger
and I want
to eat somebody up!"

But the tiger could not find
anybody to eat in the forest.

He came to a river.
He looked at himself
in the water.
He smiled and said,
"What beautiful stripes
and whiskers I have."

But then he growled again.
"I am a big, hungry,
beautiful tiger and
I want somebody good to eat.
Grrrrrr!"

Just then the tiger saw
a little green frog.

"You look like somebody
for me to eat,"
said the tiger to the frog.
"You are very small,
but you will do
for a snack.
Grrrrrr!"
And the tiger
showed his big,
white teeth.

"Oh, I would not eat me up
if I were you,"
said the frog,
"for I am the Big Boss.
I am the Big Boss
of this forest."
And the frog
puffed himself up
and smiled.

The Jump

"You do not look
like a Big Boss
to me," said the tiger.
"You look like
a little green frog
and you look like
a good snack.
I do not believe you."

"Don't believe me, then,"
   said the frog.
"But if you
   do not believe me
   and you eat me up,
   you will be in trouble."
"Trouble?" asked the tiger.
"What kind of trouble?"
"Bad trouble,"
   said the frog,
"for I am the Big Boss
   of this forest."

The tiger thought
for a minute.
His whiskers twitched.
So did his tail.
He sniffed.

"Listen," said the tiger,
"show me something
you can do better than I.
I'll bet you cannot jump
as far as I can.
We will jump
across the river.
If I jump farther than you,
I will eat you up.
If you jump farther than I,
you can jump away.
How is that?"

"All right," said the frog.

"But you will see.

No one can beat

the Big Boss!"

And they both got

ready to jump.

Just as the tiger jumped,
the little frog jumped
onto his tail.
He held on tight while
the tiger jumped
across the river.

And while the tiger jumped,
the frog took a nibble
of fur from the tiger's tail.
It was a very small nibble,
and the tiger
did not feel a thing.

Just before the tiger landed,
the frog let go.
He jumped over
the tiger's head.
He landed
in front of the tiger.
"You see," said the frog,
"I told you I would win."

"Grrrrrr!" said the tiger.
"I am angry
  because I did not win.
  And I am still hungry.
  So I will eat you anyway!"
"Oh, no you won't,"
  said the frog,
  and he jumped
  under a leaf.
  He was as green
  as the leaf.

The tiger
could not see him.
But he could hear
him laughing.

The Winner

"I bet you cannot
    spit as far as I can,"
called the frog
from under
the green leaf.

"Spitting is not nice,"
  said the tiger.
"But I am the Big Boss,"
  said the frog.
"I can do anything I like.
  And I like to spit."
"This is a silly game,"
  thought the tiger.
  But he said to the frog,
"If I win,
  will you come out
  so I can eat you up?"
"Yes," said the frog.

And the tiger spit.

He did not spit very far,

for he was thirsty.

His mouth was dry.

Then the frog spit.
He spit one inch
farther than the tiger.
He spit out
the orange and black
tiger fur
that he had nibbled
from the tiger's tail.

"What is that?"
roared the tiger,
and his tail
and whiskers twitched.

"Darn!" said the frog.
"That skinny, stringy,
  tough old tiger
  I had for dinner last night
  gave me the hiccups.
  I hiccuped all night.
  I hardly slept.
  Now I know why.
  I ate him too fast!
  You should never eat
  your dinner too fast."
  And the frog hiccuped.

"You ate a tiger?"
said the tiger,
and his teeth
began to chatter
and his eyes blinked.

"Oh, just a small one,"
said the frog.
"In fact,
now I am hungry again.
I think I will eat you!"
And he jumped out
from under the green leaf.

But the tiger
did not see him.
He did not see him because
he had run away.

The Fox

The tiger ran and ran.
He ran until
he met a fox.

"Where are you running to?"
asked the fox.
"I am not running to any place.
I am running away
from the Big Boss.
He ate a tiger for dinner
last night,
and now he is hungry again.
I do not want the Big Boss
to eat me up!"
said the tiger,
and he began to sniffle.
Then he began to cry.

"Hmmmmmm," said the fox,
"I do not know the Big Boss.
But if he eats tigers,
perhaps he eats foxes too.
Does he?"

"I do not know," said the tiger.

"Tell me about the Big Boss,"
said the fox.
"Tell me where he lives
and what he looks like.
Tell me how big he is,
and whether
he has sharp teeth."

"He lives by the river,"
said the tiger,
"and he does not look
like a Big Boss.
He looks like
a little green frog.
But he can jump farther
than I can,
and he ate
a tiger for dinner.
And he is not nice.
He spits."

"I would like to see
this Big Boss,"
said the fox.

"I am very smart
and you are very strong.
I will think up a way
to catch him,
and then
you can eat him up.
Then he will not be
the Big Boss.
He will not eat up tigers
any more—
or foxes.
Come on," said the fox.
"We will find the Big Boss."

And the tiger said,

"Well, all right.

But don't run away

and leave me.

I know what!

Tie your tail to mine.

Then you cannot run away

and leave me."

So the fox tied his tail to the tiger's.

Then the two of them
went to find
the Big Boss.

Time for Dinner

The tiger and the fox
walked to the river.

The little green frog
saw them coming.
He saw the tiger tied
to the fox's tail.
"What a silly tiger!"
he said to himself.
"Well, now I will have
some more fun!"
And the little green frog
smiled and puffed
himself up.

Then he croaked
in his loudest voice,
"Good evening, Friend Fox.
I am very glad to see you.

I have been waiting for you,
for it is time for dinner.
And what have you brought
for my dinner this evening?
What!
Is that all you could find?
Only a little pussycat
when I am so hungry?
Well, I will eat the little
pussycat for a snack.
Then I will eat you too.
For I am the Big Boss,
and I am very hungry!"

Then the frog jumped.

He jumped right

to the place

where the tiger

and the fox were standing.

The tiger ran this way.
The fox ran that way.
Each pulled the other's tail.
They pulled the knot tighter
and tighter and tighter.

Then the tiger
and the fox
ran far away.

The little green frog
sang himself a song,
ate a mosquito,
closed his eyes,
and went to sleep.

But the tiger and the fox
went on running.
They are still running
from the Big Boss.
And their tails
are still tied together.